I0830692

# REBECCA'S     SONG

## IS DEDICATED TO REBECCA WITH LOVE AND FAITH IN SPRING AWAKENINGS

# Rebecca's Song

*-Or-*

## For A child Crying

## With Scraped Knee

## By Doris T. Bush



Special Limited Edition

Illustrations by D. Corallo

Come and sit upon my knee

and I will sing a song for thee,

For thee is you and I am me

And a song is what we need, you see.

Look!  There, underneath that tree!

A rabbit sitting, do you see?

His fur is soft his feet are fast.

See him hopping in the grass?

Corello

He wasn't always there you know,

He once was hopping in the snow,

Far off where the north woods grow.

The rabbit wasn't all-alone there were other

rabbits in his home. Two brothers and a sister

too, does this sound at all like you?

Rabbit games is what they'd play,

Happy playing all the day.

And when at nighttime mother called, they

hopped into their rabbit hole.  Safe and warm

beneath the ground, mother kept them safe

and sound.

They had a back door, front door too.  Does

this sound at all like you?

Corallo

Now look again

at that same tree

And tell me

What it is you see.

High above where rabbit sat,

Tell me, do you see a cat?

There!  I see him,

Bright eyes pining

While he sits on tree limb whining,

For a friend to get him down

To the safety of the ground.

Never mind, a friend's been found.

A friend more tempting than the ground..

A bird is in that very same tree.

And happy is the cat,

You see?

He climbs along the limbs to greet her,

But if by chance he should meet her

Others of her kind will help her

Protect the nest that is the shelter

Of her baby birds or eggs

From any cat with claws and legs.

Behind the tree there is a brook

And if you try real hard

And look,

You may see some fishes swimming,

Swimming in the bubbling brook.

There beside the waters running

Sits a bullfrog; see him sunning?

Waiting for a bug to fly by, do you hear the

bug? It's coming!

I think I hear it and it's humming! Humming

very near the bullfrog.

That bug is very dear to that frog!

But never mind the bug and bullfrog.

Very near them is a big log,

Hollow from this end to that end.

A fox is hiding there

From our friend.

See him there, the dog that's barking?

We met him once when we were walking.

TigerLily
Corallo

We stopped to pet him.

His tail was wagging.

Around his neck, a collar fastened to the

leash that he was dragging.

We took him home

and watched him lapping

water from a dish,

then he was napping.